American Symbols

The Statue of Liberty

By Lloyd G. Douglas

Welcome Books™

Children's Press®
A Division of Scholastic Inc.
New York / Toronto / London / Auckland / Sydney
Mexico City / New Delhi / Hong Kong
Danbury, Connecticut

Photo Credits: Cover © Alan Schein Photography/Corbis; p. 5 © EyeWire; p. 7 © Michael S. Yamashita/Corbis; p. 9 © Gail Mooney/Corbis; pp. 11, 19 © Bettmann/Corbis; p. 13 © National Archive and Records Administration; p. 15 © Dallas and John Heaton/Corbis; p. 17 © Corbis; p. 21 © Donovan Reese /Getty Images
Contributing Editor: Jennifer Silate
Book Design: Christopher Logan

Library of Congress Cataloging-in-Publication Data

Douglas, Lloyd G.
    The Statue of Liberty/by Lloyd G. Douglas.
    p. cm. — (American symbols)
    Includes index.
    Summary: Uses easy-to-read text to introduce the Statue of Liberty as an American symbol of freedom.
    ISBN 0-516-25854-0 (lib. bdg.) — ISBN 0-516-27877-0 (pbk.)
    1. Statue of Liberty (New York, N.Y.)—Juvenile literature. 2. New York (N.Y.)—Buildings, structures, etc.—Juvenile literature. [1. Statue of Liberty (New York, N.Y.) 2. National monuments. 3. Statues. 4. New York (N.Y.)—Buildings, structures, etc.] I. Title.

F128.64.L6D68 2003
974.7'1—dc21

2002153945

Contents

The **Statue** of **Liberty** is an American **symbol**.

5

The Statue of Liberty is near New York City.

7

The Statue of Liberty is one of the largest statues ever made.

The Statue of Liberty was made in France.

France gave the statue to America in 1886.

MAISON
OUIT & BÈCHE

The Statue of Liberty was made to **celebrate** the **Declaration of Independence**.

The statue stands for America's **freedom**.

IN CONGRESS. JULY 4, 1776.

The unanimous Declaration of the thirteen united States of America.

The Statue of Liberty is holding a **tablet**.

The tablet has July 4, 1776 written on it in **Roman** numbers.

July 4, 1776 is the day the Declaration of Independence was signed.

15

A **torch** is in the statue's right hand.

The torch is meant to shine light on freedom around the world.

There is a **poem** written at the bottom of the statue.

The poem **promises** freedom to people who come to America.

18

THE NEW COLOSSUS.

NOT LIKE THE BRAZEN GIANT OF GREEK FAME,
WITH CONQUERING LIMBS ASTRIDE FROM LAND TO LAND
HERE AT OUR SEA-WASHED, SUNSET GATES SHALL STAND
A MIGHTY WOMAN WITH A TORCH, WHOSE FLAME
IS THE IMPRISONED LIGHTNING, AND HER NAME
MOTHER OF EXILES. FROM HER BEACON-HAND
GLOWS WORLD-WIDE WELCOME; HER MILD EYES COMMAND
THE AIR-BRIDGED HARBOR THAT TWIN CITIES FRAME.
"KEEP ANCIENT LANDS, YOUR STORIED POMP!"
    CRIES SHE
WITH SILENT LIPS. "GIVE ME YOUR TIRED, YOUR
    POOR,
YOUR HUDDLED MASSES YEARNING TO BREATHE FREE,
THE WRETCHED REFUSE OF YOUR TEEMING SHORE.
SEND THESE, THE HOMELESS, TEMPEST-TOST TO ME,
I LIFT MY LAMP BESIDE THE GOLDEN DOOR!"

———

THIS TABLET, WITH HER SONNET TO THE BARTHOLDI STATUE
OF LIBERTY ENGRAVED UPON IT, IS PLACED UPON THESE WALLS
IN LOVING MEMORY OF
EMMA LAZARUS
BORN IN NEW YORK CITY, JULY 22ND 1849
DIED NOVEMBER 19TH, 1887.

19

Many people visit the Statue of Liberty each year.

It is an important symbol of freedom in America.

New Words

celebrate (**sel**-uh-brate) to do something enjoyable on
  a special occasion

Declaration of Independence (dek-luh-**ray**-shuhn uhv in-di-**pen**-
  duhnss) a document declaring the freedom of the thirteen
  American colonies from British rule

freedom (**free**-duhm) being able to go where you want or do
  what you want

liberty (**lib**-ur-tee) freedom

poem (**poh**-uhm) a special way of using words that is
  different from the way we usually talk

promises (**prom**-uhss-ez) saying that you will or will not
  do something

Roman (**roh**-muhn) having to do with ancient Rome

statue (**stach**-oo) a sculpture of a person or animal made of
  stone, metal, wood, or clay

symbol (**sim**-buhl) a drawing or an object that stands for
  something else

tablet (**tab**-lit) a piece of stone with writing carved on it

torch (**torch**) a flaming light that can be carried in the hand

To Find Out More

Books
The Statue of Liberty
by Lucille Recht Penner
Random House

The Story of the Statue of Liberty
by Betsy C. Maestro
William Morrow & Company

Web Site
PBS Kids: Learning Adventures in Citizenship: The Statue of Liberty
http://www.pbs.org/wnet/newyork/laic/episode3/topic2/e3_topic2.html
Learn about how the Statue of Liberty was built on this Web site.

Index

About the Author
Lloyd G. Douglas is an editor and writer of children's books.

Reading Consultants
Kris Flynn, Coordinator, Small School District Literacy, The San Diego County
  Office of Education

Shelly Forys, Certified Reading Recovery Specialist, W.J. Zahnow Elementary
  School, Waterloo, IL

Sue McAdams, Former President of the North Texas Reading Council of the
  IRA, and Early Literacy Consultant, Dallas, TX